GreenBeard's 'Child Friendly' Vegan Verse

GreenBeard's
'Child friendly'
Vegan Verse

By

P G Holroyd

P G Holroyd

GreenBeard's 'Child Friendly' Vegan Verse

Dedicated to...

All the kids out there who choose to be vegan and all the parents who let them, for the sake of the animals, the environment and our sanity,

YOU ARE THE FUTURE!

Also, to all the SUPERHEROES who run *animal sanctuaries and rescues*, **without you there would be no hope for any of the animals.**

(The happy farm animals pictured in this book were all photographed on the following sanctuaries)

Starfield Farm Animal Sanctuary, Devon, UK

Sheep Sanctuary, North Yorkshire, UK

Maggie Fleming Animal Hospice & Karass Sanctuary, S W Scotland

Glendrick Roost Animal Welfare Centre, Scotland

P G Holroyd

Other poetry books by the same author

 **GreenBeard's Vegan Verse**

35 vegan/animal rights poems

 **Poetry of Life, The Curse of Verse**

35 poems about life, the environment and other things

Welcome to GreenBeard's
'Child Friendly' Vegan Verse

'Child friendly' means there is no swearing or graphic detail in this book, but still the poems don't beat around the bush, as in my other poem books, I tell it like it is for the animals.

This is child friendly, but not a children's book, it is written for all ages.

P G Holroyd

Contents

SHEEP 9

Pigs 11

Cows 13

CHICKENS 15

Bees 17

Animal Sanctuary 19

No Difference 21

Mother Earth 23

Someone 24

Cruelty free 25

Friends not Food 26

Firework Night 29

Trick or Treat 31

History Lesson 32

Wildlife 34

VEGAN WARS 35

AVEGANGERS 36

Adopt, Love, Keep 37

Fox hunting is wrong 39

 Please don't buy that 40

Vegan kids 42

GreenBeard's 'Child Friendly' Vegan Verse

Vegan Parents on holiday 44

My Life 45

Day at the Zoo... 46

Vegan Future... 49

Do you want to be vegan? 50

Tomato.. 52

Potato 53

Onion 54

Beans... 55

Green Vegetables 56

Remember your roots.. 57

FRUIT 58

VEGAN junk food 59

FOR THE CHILDREN 60

P G Holroyd

SHEEP

GreenBeard's 'Child Friendly' Vegan Verse

SHEEP

Oh my goodness, what a lot of sheep, you're some kind of Little Bo Peep

With geese and chickens and a cock-a-doodle-doo, some pigs, some goats and a shed full of poo

You rescued them from a far worse fate, arriving here in an awful state

You gave them love and showed you care, which in this world is far too rare

Now they're all happy and feel secure, you've changed their lives to something pure

You join in all their sheepy games, and gave them lots of floral names

There's *Iris, Daffodil, Tulip* and *Rose, Petunia, Hyacinth*, and little *Primrose*

Buttercup, Lavender, Pansy and *Lilly*, and *Marigold* and *Daisy* are very silly

They're so, so lucky to be with you, protected by a love so true

You feed them well and let them roam, **thank you**, for giving them a home

P G Holroyd

PIGS

GreenBeard's 'Child Friendly' Vegan Verse

Pigs

Please see past my snout and take a good look in my eyes

You'll see my cleverness, and my beauty in disguise

I'm no different from a dog if I'm given half a chance

Next time that you see me please take a second glance

I don't deserve the labels that most people think I am

I'm not a piece of bacon, neither am I

pork nor ham

I'm just a friendly animal, longing to be free

So, if you ever see a pig, please be nice to me

P G Holroyd

COWS

GreenBeard's 'Child Friendly' Vegan Verse

Cows

Big and square and beautiful

Black and white, or brown

You see them in the countryside

You don't see them in town

They can play like giant puppies

If they're free to do their thing

When they're happy you can see it

You can feel the joy they bring

They're animals, they have a life

They're not a piece of meat

Their milk is for their babies

It's not for us to eat

Show them that we love them

Show them that we care

Let them know that there aren't

Human Monsters everywhere

P G Holroyd

CHICKENS

GreenBeard's 'Child Friendly' Vegan Verse

CHICKENS

They're so much more than nuggets, don't call them 'finger Lickin'

Each one's an individual, a living, breathing chicken

They all have personalities the same as you or I

They don't like pain and suffering,

why would they want to die?

Please see them all as someone, and not a piece of meat

Their lives are worth much more than a

ninety-nine pence treat

You won't be missing out if you choose plant-based instead

In fact, you'll both be better off as the

chickens won't be dead

P G Holroyd

BEES

GreenBeard's 'Child Friendly' Vegan Verse

Bes

What do you know about bees? Tell me what's the buzz?

Did you know that a world without bees is also a world without us?

Those tiny colourful creatures, buzzing from flower to plant

Pollinating the world and keeping it growing on a scale that humans just can't

I don't mean the ones that people control in order to steal all their honey

Those bees are bred for only one purpose, to make somebody some money

It's the natural bees that keep the world going, the **wild honeybees and the bumble**

If someone so small is such a big deal, all we can feel is humble

So leave them some food, let the wild flowers grow and they'll help to feed us in return

Pass on this knowledge to all who you know, it's a lesson we all need to learn

P G Holroyd

ANIMAL SANCTUARY

GreenBeard's 'Child Friendly' Vegan Verse

Animal Sanctuary

Sanctuary means a place safe from harm, in this case for animals born on the farm

Saved from their fate and brought to the rescue and if you eat meat they were rescued from you

Sanctuary means a place full of glee, somewhere they're loved, cared for and free

Free to go oink, baaa, cluck or moo and if you drink dairy they were rescued from you

Sanctuary is the place they call home, barns they can sleep in and land they can roam

Escaped from the things they were once forced to do and if you eat eggs they're escaping from you

Sanctuaries run by people who care, every day in all weather, always they're there

Help if you can, give a fiver or two because if you're not vegan they were rescued from you

Sanctuaries are places in desperate need of volunteers and money for animal feed

I like to help out when I have some time free;

Because before I went vegan ***they were rescued from me***

P G Holroyd

No Difference

20

GreenBeard's 'Child Friendly' Vegan Verse

No Difference

Can you tell when a dog is happy?

Can you tell when they're feeling sad?

Is the fear that they feel any less real

Than the feelings that you might have had?

Why would it be any different

For a pig or a sheep or a cow?

Or a chicken or fish, they all have the same wish

To survive, do you understand now?

So many species all made the same way

With our love, our hopes, and our fears

We're all flesh and blood, not pieces of wood

Please don't be the cause of our tears

P G Holroyd

GreenBeard's 'Child Friendly' Vegan Verse

Mother Earth

Since the day of your birth your home's been on **Earth**

Shared with every other race

And just like the others you're *born with two mothers*

Both are your world in one place

Treat them both with respect, please try not to neglect

Either one, that's the challenge you face

And the same goes for all *creatures large and small*

Give them your loving embrace

We all have the same worth to our old **Mother Earth**

All her children floating through space

So, *all Earthlings unite*, keep doing what's right

As she's not someone we can replace

P G Holroyd

Someone

ALL animals are SOMEONE, that cannot be denied

Look into their eyes, *you can see someone inside*

You'll see them looking back at you, you'll see how much they've cried

For a billion other animals, the *'someones' that have died*

Don't think of them as *'something'*, never try to hide

That all animals are SOMEONE, it cannot be denied

GreenBeard's 'Child Friendly' Vegan Verse

Cruelty free

Check before you buy, make sure the label that you see

Is of the **leaping bunny**, or at least it says it's

cruelty-free

Don't pay for products if they've

used animals to test

Only buying things that don't hurt anyone is best

Get to know which products that you buy are

safe for use

And then you'll know that *you don't pay for*

animal abuse

P G Holroyd

Friends not Food

When you think of animals, what goes through your mind?

Do you think of them as food because your taste buds leave you blind?

When you search inside your heart what emotion do you find?

Are you happy being cruel or do you see yourself as kind?

If meat is what you choose to eat, **animals must die**

It's bits of their dead bodies in your burger or your pie

You're paying for their suffering every time you buy

That sausage or that sandwich, that's no word of a lie

If dairy milk is what you want a **baby's life will end**

He's not allowed to drink his mother's milk, **let's not pretend**

The cheese you buy will pay for **cruelty you can't defend**

The cow becomes your victim when **she could have been *your friend***

GreenBeard's 'Child Friendly' Vegan Verse

If eggs are what you ask for then chickens end up dead

When all you had to do was ask for something else instead

Aren't their lives worth more than a filling for your bread?

Think about your choices, try to use your head

Animals can feel like you, animals can think

Animals don't want to be a thing you eat or drink

Animals are friends not food, don't wash them down the sink

Learn where your food comes from, **try to make that link**

P G Holroyd

GreenBeard's 'Child Friendly' Vegan Verse

Firework Night

It's firework night so lots of bright explosives in the air
But do it right in case it might give animals a scare
In the night it's quite a sight, watching with your gang
But have the light without the fright,
the flash without the bang

Fireworks aren't toys and all that noise will terrify your pets
Girls and boys can still get joy without the screaming jets
It causes strife to wildlife; some people get upset
On sanctuaries and farms it causes animals to fret

So please be fair and if you care, in countryside or town
Stand and stare, enjoy the glare but keep the volume down
Have your fun and when it's done, go home to your beds
Knowing all the animals aren't screaming in their heads

P G Holroyd

GreenBeard's 'Child Friendly' Vegan Verse

Trick or Treat

Wandering from street to street, fancy dress from head to feet, joining up with friends you meet

HAPPY HALLOWEEN

Horror is the theme tonight, hoping that you'll get a fright, animals are scared alright

HAPPY HALLOWEEN

Asking for a trick or treat, maybe lots of chewy sweets, did you know they're made of meat?

HAPPY HALLOWEEN

Dairy chocolate bars taste great, can't recall how much you ate, shame about the cows, too late!

HAPPY HALLOWEEN

A trick for them a treat for you, it's not as if you really knew the cruelty we put them through

HAPPY HALLOWEEN

The scary things were all pretend at least for you and all your friends but cows are suffering, no end

HAPPY HALLOWEEN

Now you know and if you care, when you come around next year ask for plant-based treats to share

HAPPY HALLOWEEN

P G Holroyd

History Lesson

In days of old the tales are told of victories in war

Although it's hard to understand what they were fighting for

The stories say the victors were all wholesome to the core

And once they'd won there wasn't any evil anymore

But for them to get the win meant many innocents must die

The soldiers did as they were told, believing every lie

They blindly followed orders, without the question "why?"

Then later with their memories they'd sit alone and cry

In days gone by it's hard to try and justify our deeds

Uprooting whole communities, like gardeners do with weeds

Keeping them in chains, ignoring basic human needs

It's shameful looking back to see the way our history reads

Even now the colour of a skin is causing fights

Like a global game of chess with opposing blacks and whites

And still some men think women aren't allowed to reach their heights

Our ignorant societies refusing equal rights

GreenBeard's 'Child Friendly' Vegan Verse

A history yet to come is the one we're living now

For all beings of the future we can change their past somehow

Not only for the people, but for a ***pig, a sheep, a cow***

We shouldn't be confined to what the law says they allow

So, when it comes to history be on the right side of it

Don't judge someone worthless because their face doesn't fit

Having some compassion and the courage to commit

Will make history we can be proud of, so never ever quit!

The way we've treated animals is a thing of constant shame

Imagine if another species treated us the same

So many creatures better off before the humans came

The only way to change is to accept that we're to blame

The history that we're making now is better for us all

It's the only way to stop our planet's impending downfall

To be kind to every being that can *fly, swim, walk or crawl*

A vegan human history is what our future should recall

P G Holroyd

Wildlife

It's lovely to see when an animal's free, the birds in the sky and the fish in the sea

Hedgehogs and badgers out in the wild should cheer up the heart of any adult or child

The squirrels and foxes, the deer in the woods, the frogs and the rabbits, the bees on the buds

All of those animals living their lives, so high are their flights, so deep are their dives

Making their homes in a natural way, if only humans could leave them that way

But they all have a predator after their blood, with nets in the ocean and guns in the wood

Hunting and fishing and culling and kills, hungering for **all the** blood that it spills

With huge packs of hounds and a murderous cry, rods in **the** rivers and shots in the sky

Those poor wild animals can never be free until the world goes vegan, ***obviously***

GreenBeard's 'Child Friendly' Vegan Verse

VEGAN WARS

Not long ago in a galaxy not far away, *animals were hurt and killed every single day*

Human beings turning to the dark side without thinking, reluctant to acknowledge all the blood that they were drinking

A few brave rebels, **The Vegan Order**, were their only hope, they had to fight the dark side to help the others cope

They defended all the animals, united with their force, but so few against the Empire they had little chance of course

So overwhelming was the darkness that the Vegans nearly broke, **but their conviction was too strong**, and in time, others awoke

Now the *Vegan Order* grows and the Empire's running scared, they know Vegans won't stop until every life is spared

As the dark side is diminishing, a bit more every day and more people are realising that there's a better way

The time is getting closer when the Empire will surrender and the world will know that **VEGAN** just means

'ANIMAL DEFENDER'

P G Holroyd

AVEGANGERS

At last a team of **vegan superheroes** emerge

To stop animal oppression and to end the carnist purge

A**VEGAN**GERS assemble, it's time to do your thing

Go rescue all the sentient souls, go stop the suffering

Iron Man and Thor go and break down all the walls

Of *slaughterhouses everywhere until the last one falls*

Get the Hulk worked up into one of his big rages

Then set him loose on *factory farms, smashing all the cages*

Captain and Black Widow go and **get the animals out**

With Hawkeye as your backup your success won't be in doubt

Nick Fury and his S.H.I.E.L.D. have arranged a safer place

Far away from humans on a world in outer space

Every species used by man will be *safely out of range*

They'll travel through a window conjured up by Dr Strange

Safe to live their lives with no more suffering and fear

And humans will live on plants in a better world down here

GreenBeard's 'Child Friendly' Vegan Verse

Adopt, Love, Keep

Do you want to live with a dog or a cat?

Or maybe a rabbit, a gerbil, a rat?

Don't go to the pet shop, you don't need to pay

Adopt from a rescue, that's the best way

There are thousands of animals with nowhere to live

Abandoned by people with no love to give

If you buy from a pet shop you're giving them money

To breed another cat, dog or bunny

Give a home to the homeless, cheer up the sad

Show them the best home that they've ever had

P G Holroyd

Fox hunting is wrong

GreenBeard's 'Child Friendly' Vegan Verse

Fox hunting is wrong

Privileged people in red and black

Please open up your hearts a crack

You train your dogs and ride your horse

To kill a fox without remorse

You have your life and they have theirs

Why would you think that no one cares

When you go hunting just for fun

And force your animals to run

The foxes' lives belong to them

What makes you think you can condemn

Them all to death, it's not your call

You don't seem very nice at all

P G Holroyd

Please don't buy that

Don't buy those burgers mum, they used to be a cow

If you buy those burgers it will make us have a row

There's no way I will eat them, I'm telling you right now

Please let's choose the vegan ones instead

Don't buy those sausages, they caused a pig to die

If you buy those sausages it's going to make me cry

There are so many other types of sausages to buy

Please let's choose the vegan ones instead

Don't buy that jacket dad, the skin is from a cow

If you buy that jacket you're condoning it somehow

Wearing it is not something my conscience will allow

Please let's choose a vegan one instead

Don't buy me that woolly hat, you know I'm not a fool

That pompom is from rabbit fur, it's horrible and cruel

I read about it from a library book I saw in school

Please let's find a vegan one instead

GreenBeard's 'Child Friendly' Vegan Verse

Don't buy that chocolate nan, the milk came from a cow

She made it for her baby, and they're both crying now

I won't eat dairy products, I've made myself a vow

Please let's buy the vegan ones instead

Don't buy that birthday cake it's made with eggs and honey

The bees and chickens suffer, it really isn't funny

If you buy that cake for me it's just a waste of money

Please let's buy a vegan one instead

Don't buy that shampoo, I wouldn't use it on my hair

It's been tested on animals, it really isn't fair

If you want to get me something show me that you care

Please let's find a vegan one instead

P G Holroyd

Vegan kids

What do you want for breakfast kids? What shall I cook?

Some sausages with bacon, and eggs, come take a look

Or maybe just some porridge made with thick and creamy milk

It used to be your favourite, whipped up as smooth as silk

No, never again will we help you kill a pig

Or cause the pain of chickens our conviction is too big

That milk is made by mothers, it's to feed a baby cow

We're only ever going to choose the vegan options now

What do you want for lunch kids? What shall I do?

How about fish fingers, does that sound good to you?

Or how about an omelette, would that hit the spot

That would work, along with chips and beans would it not?

The chips and beans are good, but you know we don't eat fish

We never want to see another carcass on our dish

And no more eggs, we need to get it through to you somehow

We're only ever going to have the vegan options now

GreenBeard's 'Child Friendly' Vegan Verse

What do you want for dinner kids? What shall I make?

I could go to the butchers for some lovely juicy steak

Or shall I get some burgers and we'll have a barbeque

Or maybe buy some mince and cook a really meaty stew

Not a chance, you know we don't eat animals anymore

We learnt the truth a year ago, we're vegan to the core

We'll never help you pay towards the killing of a cow

We're only ever going to eat the vegan options now

P G Holroyd

Vegan Parents on holiday

Mum, Dad, come and look, there's donkeys on the beach

Can I go and have a ride or are you going to preach?

> **Sorry babe, you know we don't like animal abuse**
>
> **Those donkeys don't do that by choice, there's really no excuse**

We've walked around for ages, can't we ride a horse and cart?

I'm tired and I've got blisters on my feet for a start

> **That poor horse is forced to pull the heavy cart all day**
>
> **We refuse to contribute to slavery, no way!**

Well, can I have a photo with that monkey over there?

All my friends have got one, why can't I? It isn't fair

> **It's not fair on the monkey, he's kept locked up at night**
>
> **And treated like a money-making tool, it's just not right**

Can we get some fish 'n' chips, and maybe some ice cream?

Nan would let me have some, so why are you so mean?

> **Let's look for vegan options, there's plenty we can find**

We're not mean, in time you'll see the truth, *we're being kind*

GreenBeard's 'Child Friendly' Vegan Verse

My Life

Animal lover, cruelty free

Empty the cages, let them all be

Adopt, don't shop, give them a voice

Woke from the Matrix, made the right choice

Eat only plant-based, wear my own skin

The rest of my life is about to begin

Don't ride them, don't make them pull a cart

See them as someone, open my heart

No SeaWorld, no animal testing

Peaceful animal rights protesting

Don't eat meat or eggs or dairy

Vegetables are much less scary

Animals are not ours to use

No factory farms or breeding zoos

The way I'm living makes me smile

Because I love my VEGAN lifestyle

P G Holroyd

Day at the Zoo

The day that we went to the ZOO,

there was really a heck of a queue

We all had to wait 'til they opened the gate

I was dying to get to the loo

We went to the elephants first,

so sad that our hearts nearly burst

They stood in the mud and didn't look good

I'm not sure it could have been worse

The gorilla was next on the list,

he was banging the ground with his fist

And to my surprise what I saw in his eyes

Was a tenderness hard to resist

Then came the lions in cages,

a whole range of differing ages

Their instincts gone stale from their time in the jail

Like books that had lost half their pages

GreenBeard's 'Child Friendly' Vegan Verse

There were tigers and other big cats,

hippos and penguins and bats

The buffalo herd looked very absurd

Crammed into concreted flats

The zebras were in with the giraffes,

the hyenas had all lost their laughs

The crocodile's tears confirmed my worst fears

And dead animals were served in the cafes

All those prisoners serving their time,

though they hadn't committed a crime

The old ones beguiled after life in the wild

The young ones never reaching their prime

It occurred to me after we left,

we were feeling so sad and bereft

It just isn't fair, they shouldn't be there

They are all hapless victims of theft

P G Holroyd

Vegan future

GreenBeard's 'Child Friendly' Vegan Verse

Vegan Future

At some time in our future, when vegans win at last
The horror stories told to kids will be about our past
They won't believe the tales about the *things we used to eat*
As mythical as unicorns, the eggs and milk and meat

It will sound so medieval, all the things we used to do
Even though it's all still happening now, in 2022
They'll hear the tales of **women's rights and human slavery**
And how the laws were changed because of **selfless bravery**

They'll wonder how the leaders of the world could be so cruel
And why the people *always voted for another fool*
They'll be relieved that things like that don't happen anymore
And that animal equality has now become the law

The planet's so much better off than it used to be
When factory farming threatened to destroy our destiny
And the animals themselves are living in a better place
Now that they share the world with a kinder human race

P G Holroyd

Do you want to be vegan?

Do you know what it means to be vegan?

Do you know what vegans believe?

Do you know what they eat?

Do you know what they wear?

Do you know what they try to achieve?

To be vegan means that they *care for all life*

They believe in an animal's worth

They don't eat them or wear them

Or use them or hurt them

They're loved from the day of their birth

It's not so much about things that they eat

More about things that they don't

So if you want to be vegan

Make up your own mind

And either you will or you won't

GreenBeard's 'Child Friendly' Vegan Verse

FOOD

P G Holroyd

Tomato

The tomato has issues, it's very confused

It's the subject of a dispute

It's always treated like a vegetable

Even though it knows it's a fruit

It's a very versatile kind of food

Makes a lovely soup or a sauce

But if it sneaks into the fruit bowl

It's ejected immediately, of course

For a curry, it's chopped up and spiced

In a salsa it's probably diced

For a fresh salad sandwich it's sliced

But in a fruit salad, it's not very nice

Outcast among its own fruity kind

But it's not as sad as you think

Because it's welcomed by almost all other foods

And even by some other drinks

GreenBeard's 'Child Friendly' Vegan Verse

Potato

There's not a veg more versatile than the humble spud
No matter how you cook it, the taste is always good
You can even leave the skin on if you clean off all the mud
The perfect thing to share a dinner with a Yorkshire pud

On warm days a potato salad helps to cool you down
On cold days leave the jacket on to take away your frown
A topping for a cottage pie, all crisp and golden brown
And chips will go with anything, really go to town

Chop them up and boil them, creamy mash is nice
Lovely baked as wedges and covered in a spice
With a curry, half 'n' half, chips along with rice
Sautéed as a topping, you can even bake them twice

Cheap and cheerful, red or white, even get them sweet
Fully loaded fries, have them curly as a treat
The best all-round accompaniment for any food they meet
And you can get them anywhere, a shop on every street

P G Holroyd

Onion

The onion's a funny'un, I really don't know why

Peel the skin and breathe it in and it'll make you cry

But when it's cooked it has you hooked, especially when you fry

In a sandwich, a stew, on pizza too, or cook it in a pie

When you tear its many layers you see into its soul

And then you slice, or maybe dice and fill a salad bowl

It's tasty raw, you'll want some more, but you've scored an own goal

Your breath will smell and, truth to tell, your heartburn takes a toll

It's flavoury in savoury, but terrible in sweet

Big mistake to use in cake, you don't want that to eat

But in a flan, oh yes you can, a taste that's hard to beat

That's shallot, cold or hot, it's a culinary treat

GreenBeard's 'Child Friendly' Vegan Verse

Beans

A good healthy dinner is one full of beans, perfect for adults and toddlers and teens

Smothered in sauce and sitting on toast are the beans that the British enjoy the most

But there's so many other types waiting for you to have in a pie or a soup or a stew

There's kidney and pinto, chickpea and runner, red beans and black beans and lentils are gonna

Fill you with protein and build you up strong, the black-eyed peas might sing you a song

Adzuki, borlotti, the big beans called butter, but don't eat the has-beens you find in the gutter

Cannellini and mung, or soy if you'd rather, if you want to know more ask edamame or fava

So get your pulses racing with beans on your plate

And enjoy all the fumes from legumes you just ate

P G Holroyd

Green Vegetables

A big shout out for the Brussel sprout, the cabbage and the kale

Broccoli and spinach are vegetables which will improve your health without fail

Eating your greens is always a means to improving the strength of your heart

Have the belief that a vegetable leaf will always be a good start

Lettuce and cress you can eat to excess, top up your salad with greens

Be sure to say please when offered some peas or a lovely big pile of green beans

Packed full of vitamins make sure you fit em in most of your meals of the day

Eat every bit to keep yourself fit and chase the diseases away

GreenBeard's 'Child Friendly' Vegan Verse

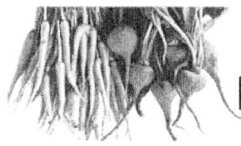

Remember your roots

The plants that we eat are nutritious and sweet, the stems and the flowers and shoots

But there's more to be found, the ones underground, remember to dig up the roots

The turnip and swede provide a good feed, packed full of fibre and iron

Celery and beet are good ones to eat, when you go to the shops you should buy em

There's potatoes of course but try not to force too many carbs in one go

Carrot, parsnip, onion and garlic know how to put on a good show

If you want to know others go ask your mothers, they know the best ones to cook

Or go to the yard an' dig up the garden, see for yourself, have a look

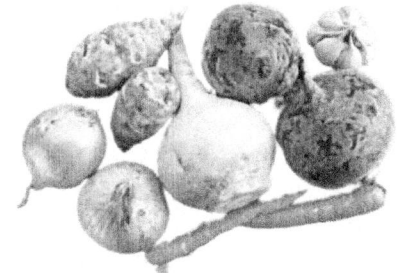

Holroyd

FRUIT

When you want some pudding add some colour to your dish

Zesty, juicy and sweet

Peeled and chopped, eat them as you wish

So many fruits to eat

Flambeed banana, apple in a pie

Strawberries and cream

Rhubarb crumble, give pineapple a try

Live the fruity dream

Oranges and lemons, grapefruit if you dare

Topped with a glace cherry

Watermelon, mango or grab a juicy pear

Even blow a raspberry

Pomegranate, apricot, sucking on a peach

Be sure to try a plum

Black and blue berries and grapes on the beach

All bought by your mum

GreenBeard's 'Child Friendly' Vegan Verse

VEGAN junk food

Vegans only taste food that's plant-based, for that we don't need to be wealthy

But some plants nowadays are processed in ways

That isn't, in truth very healthy

We have burgers and pies, pizzas and fries, foods that are tempting and tasty

Enjoy as you chew it but don't overdo it

Or you'll end up all bloated and pasty

All kinds of cheese, Hummus? Yes please! So much to fill up your bread

It's nice now and then but you're better off when

You choose something healthy instead

Have something sweet or a savoury treat, it's not as if it's a crime

But think of your health when you look on the shelf

Eat fruit and veg most of the time

P G Holroyd

FOR THE CHILDREN

All you boys and all you girls

Learn about the vegan world

Better for the animals, and for you

Better for your planet too

Tell your mum and tell your dad

That eating animals is bad

Being vegan means you're clever

A VEGAN WORLD WIL LIVE FOREVER!

GreenBeard's 'Child Friendly' Vegan Verse

FOR THE ANIMALS

Follow me on Facebook, Instagram and YouTube

Facebook page; P G Holroyd, Poetry

Instagram; pgholroydpoetry

YouTube channels; GreenBeard (Vegan Poet)

        P G Holroyd, Poetry

P G Holroyd

Printed in Great Britain
by Amazon